NIGHT
Light

To Kathy,

Thanks for your
support!

Kim Steadman

30 Day Devotional

NIGHT
Light

Kim Strootman

TATE PUBLISHING
AND ENTERPRISES, LLC

This book is designed to provide accurate and authoritative information with regard to the subject matter covered. This information is given with the understanding that neither the author nor Tate Publishing, LLC is engaged in rendering legal, professional advice. Since the details of your situation are fact dependent, you should additionally seek the services of a competent professional.

The opinions expressed by the author are not necessarily those of Tate Publishing, LLC.

Published by Tate Publishing & Enterprises, LLC
127 E. Trade Center Terrace | Mustang, Oklahoma 73064 USA
1.888.361.9473 | www.tatepublishing.com

Tate Publishing is committed to excellence in the publishing industry. The company reflects the philosophy established by the founders, based on Psalm 68:11,
"The Lord gave the word and great was the company of those who published it."

Published in the United States of America

ISBN: 978-1-63367-746-3
Religion / Christian Life / Devotional
15.05.06

Acknowledgments

I would like to give special thanks to my husband, Mike, my daughter, Ashley, and son, Devin, for their loving support. Particular gratitude goes to Lexie for her extraordinary photography work and Cathy for her exceptional talent in creating the book cover.

Day 1

Just like a photo album, memories of our past snap through our mind reminding us of all the times God was there for us, even when we were running from Him. Remember the story in the Bible of that one lost sheep that Jesus went after? There were ninety-nine others safely in the sheep's pen, but His concern was for the lost one. It is so comforting to know that when we were that "one lost sheep," God came looking for us. Matthew 18:12 (NIV) says, "What do you think? If a man owns a hundred sheep, and one of them wanders away, will he not leave the ninety-nine on the hills and go to look for the one that wandered off?".

The Unseen Hand

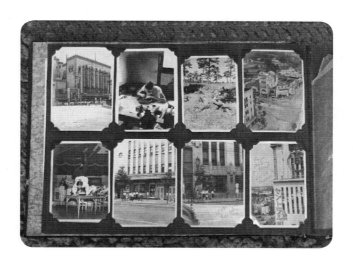

Looking back upon my life, some photos fill my mind;
memories of time that's past, some sad and some are kind.
Many snapshots are reflections of mistakes I've made,
leaving God behind me caused my path to go astray.
Flipping through the photos I see faces of the past,
manifold emotions but God's picture was the last.
Seemed I had forgotten all He brought me through
you see,
staring at each picture was a hand surrounding me!
Chills ran through my body, and I prayed through
bitter tears,

"Jesus, why did you stay even in rebellious years?"
Answering He said, "I've waited years to hear you call,
I loved you even when you thought your world would
surely fall.
"Always just a prayer away I cried to hear your voice,
now that you're returning home all Heaven will rejoice!"
Slowly laying photos down my life is now complete,
God is in each picture turning bitter into sweet.
If your life is broken and there's no where left to run,
there's just one solution He is Jesus Christ, God's Son.

Day 2

Our relationship with God is a lot like a dance—you have a leader and a follower. You both must know the moves in order to flow gracefully on the dance floor. I attended a hangar dance recently. The dance took place at my husband's place of employment in the airplane hangar. The music and a lot of the dresses were reminiscent of the big band era. We saw every dance possible from that era being done, especially swing.

An older gentleman, who was a terrific dancer, invited one of the ladies from our table to dance. He showed her how the dances were done, teaching her what each movement meant. Who knew that even the slightest turn of the hand had a meaning? Our *dance* on Earth as we walk with God is much like this. Everything we're involved in has meaning and training for our lives—classes we attend, jobs, etc. Many times we are trying to get out of the current place we are at to move on to the next phase thinking it will be bigger and better. Take time to realize that God has a plan for you right where you're at now. Look for the roses among the thorns of each day!

Holy Dance

Living in the drudgery of guilt, remorse and sin,
wanting to get out instead of getting deeper in.
One hand on my shoulder and the other hand in mine,
God asked me to dance with Him—His touch was so sublime.
Letting Him begin to lead, the chains began to break,
feeling I could breathe again, the ground began to quake.
Gliding on the floor, I noticed air was getting lighter,
sins' strong grip had lifted, and I felt God's cleansing power.

Twirling me He showed me some new steps along the way,
some moves were much harder but determined—I did stay.
Wouldn't trade my partner and my dancing broke the fetters,
I realized what I must do is simply know Him better.

Kim Strootman

Day 3

After the death of a great public figure, I was watching the memorial, which was an exquisite display of nature and splendor with many noted speakers. Though we were all stunned by the untimely death and grieved for the family, I was more grieved by this unknown question: where had this person ended up in eternity? I may never know the answer to that question but was stirred to be sure those I know are ready to step into eternity.

As time marched on and I attended other memorials of friends that passed away, I realized how easy it could be to glorify good acts of those who lived but leave out mentioning God at our funerals. Don't get me wrong I love the idea of celebrating a person's life instead of the "old-school funeral," which morbidly focuses on their death. We cannot overlook the clear opportunity to preach what we really believe about eternity. Christian memorials need to say so! This scripture spoke to me concerning this very thing, "If only for this life we have hope in Christ, we are to be pitied more than all men. But Christ has indeed been raised from the dead, the first fruits of those who have fallen asleep. For since death came through a man, the resurrection of the dead comes also through a man. For as in Adam all die, so in Christ all will be made alive" (1 Cor. 15:19–22, NIV).

Memorial to Memorials

As time marches forward there's a pattern I can see,
our approach to death is hiding noted human need.
In times past a funeral reasoned heaven's question,
now we have "memorials" where God's not even mentioned.
Memorials are great if you have lived a life for God,
but if a person hasn't, can life after be ignored?
Today I'm very grieved because the world has lost a friend,
however all they mentioned was that he was a good man.

Much was said today on how he chose to live his life,
not a word was mentioned about God or Jesus Christ.
Yes, he was a good man to all animals and men,
but Christ is what's required of you when life comes to an end.
May we be wiser stewards in the age in which we're living,
to preach the gospel of our Lord while we're alive and breathing.
Tomorrow's just another day—memorials will be done,
will they say at the next one that they knew God's only Son?

Kim Strootman

Day 4

Have you ever noticed when you're driving you can't only trust your mirrors and windows to see if the coast is clear to change lanes? You have to turn your head and look. Many times, I have been ready to change lanes, looked in my mirrors, and right as I turned my head to do a last-minute check, I noticed a car right beside me in that lane! It's really scary when that happens, but these last-minute checks save you from disaster. Life is like that: sometimes we are blinded by things we don't see creeping up next to us. If we're not careful we can get sideswiped by things we are not prepared for.

Blind Spot

Every driver knows there is a blind
spot you can't see,
it's just a little section where the
danger's sure to be.
You really must be careful that you check
it every time
or you could end up in a wreck that's
why its name is *blind*!
If you could see it perfectly,
you wouldn't get in trouble,
but oh it's just a little spot that's sure
to bring you double!

Lord help us see our blind spots while
we're walking through this life,
for many times it's just too late when
we see its strife.
Show us how to see these things that
try to steal our walk,
and let us stop and look before the
lanes we try to cross!

Day 5

It is amazing to think about creation; God spoke and things began to happen! There was a distinct plan for man in God's creation. He chose to form us in His own image and likeness and placed us here to rule over the rest of the things He created. Ponder the absolute wonder of that moment in time when God bent down and formed man from the earth. He used His own breath to start man as a living being—amazing. Consider this Bible verse, "The Lord God formed man of the dust of the ground, and breathed into his nostrils the breath of life, and man became a living being" (Gen. 2:7, NKJV).

Breath of Life

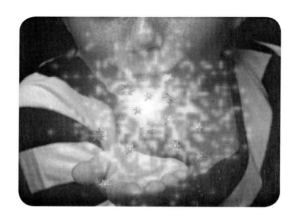

Intimate moment during creation,
God took time in man's formation.
Bent down and gathered dust from this sod,
with His hand He formed us in the image of God.
Then God did something deeply personal,
He breathed His own breath into man's nostrils.
This is how man first came to life,
not from words, loud crashes or light.
So get deeply personal in your walk with Christ,
Take time in His word—let Him into your life.
He'll lead you and guide you along life's path,
then you'll meet Him in heaven when you draw that last breath.

Day 6

There are many people in life that have great talent. Finding the balance of humility, perfecting the gift, and a willingness to serve others with it is a must. As we mature in Christ and use our gifts and talents, pride is extracted from our lives. We begin to become something beautiful like a flower that is changing from a closed bud to a perfectly open flower.

When we employ our talents to help others, we become an instrument of healing. We all have seen famous, talented people that have allowed things to creep into their lives and destroy that beautiful gift they possess. It's a very tragic sight, but we have also seen famous people that have used their gifts to help others and kept themselves from being tainted by the world. That's an outstanding sight to see. By keeping our eyes on Jesus, we realize that everything we possess is no comparison to Him!

Kim Strootman

Gifts and Talents

Gifts can be polished, hit the mark every time,
talents forged to be perfectly in rhyme.
Without a walk of purity to accompany the two,
it's like ground without rain or morning without dew.
May I never be comfortable using gifts and talents,
without a close walk with Jesus to keep me in balance.
My life's not my own—You're truly my Lord,
lead me to be still with you feed me from your Word.

Day 7

This poem was written while I was working a full-time job, trying to write a book, and being a good child of God, wife, and mother. Life can really keep you running! I don't know about you, but I often feel like I'm failing miserably at what I should be doing the best. As time went on, I began to evaluate my life and figure out why I wasn't accomplishing the things I was put here to do and using all my time doing other things. It's really hard when you have to work full-time: there just seemingly isn't enough time in a day. Before you know it, days turn into weeks, weeks turn into months, and months turn into years. For me, I took a good hard look at what I could change in my off time. Is it time for you to reevaluate your priorities too?

Full-Time

Pinned up here inside this box, I'm torn between two sides,
one that says, "Just stay the course" the other, "Run and hide!"
Constantly stretched to do more chores to equal lukewarm pay,
my life is in a Vortex of no time for my own day.
Creative juices dry up while I'm working 8–5,
desperately wanting to get out and have a little life.
When am I supposed to muse, reflect or sit and write?
Even time with nature has taken wing in flight!

Maintaining home is nonexistent and so my guilt's increased,
Clean house? Clean Clothes? A home-cooked meal?
These things have almost ceased!
I tell myself, "I'm useful" then mistakes I made are mentioned,
Quite mad is the one who finds their worth wrapped up
in a pension!
I must evaluate "off time"—my soul's in need of healing,
it's time to focus on what can change instead of what
work's stealing.

Day 8

Friends are a treasure in life. We all want friends that are there for us no matter what life holds. This poem came from a realization that when hard times came for me, there were some girlfriends and sisters that were there. Sometimes you have to look around in the middle of your "life storm" to see who is still standing beside you. This is a tribute to friends who are there for us through thick and thin. Proverbs 17:17 (NIV) says, "A friend loves at all times, and a brother is born for times of adversity."

Friends

Friends are God's gift to us; partners in life,
sharing hope; giving life spice.
A friend is always there with a smile,
will sit silently with you for a long while.
A friend will stick with you until the end,
these are the reasons I call you my friend.

Day 9

No matter what your past is, we all stand the same before God—spotless. He sees us only through the blood of Jesus. Once we have accepted Jesus as our Savior, old things are passed away, and all things become new! The Bible has this to say about this subject, "In all this you greatly rejoice, though now for a little while you may have had to suffer grief in all kinds of trials. These have come so that your faith—of greater worth than gold, which perishes even though refined by fire—may be proved genuine and may result in praise, glory and honor when Jesus Christ is revealed" (1 Pet. 1:6–7, TNIV).

Gold

Scorned by women rejected by men,
this is where your new life begins.
Though this cup is bitter like an icy cold blast,
God's cleaning up messes and healing your past.
For now learn the lessons this season brings,
one day it will end, again you will sing.
Don't give up the fight, don't let yourself fail,
stand your ground and put up your sail!

Be sure the day's coming, if you'll pass the test,
the sting will be lifted and lighten your chest.
So if you are fighting a tumultuous battle,
friend, I've been there, I know that you're frazzled!
God loves you, He's with you and wants you
to know,
everything's hopeful, you're turning to Gold!

Kim Strootman

Day 10

For several years, I worked in the church drama department. Every Easter before Jesus walked down the aisle carrying His cross, I was in charge of the Passion scene where Jesus was beaten, bloodied and bruised, and was about to walk to Calvary. I had to check my stock to be sure I had everything I needed for each performance. One day after doing that, I was leaving the church, and this poem came to me. I had been to numerous practices and performances for that drama and was saturated by the great price God the Father and the Son paid for us. I was working on a drama about Jesus's death when I wrote a poem about His first coming. It became very clear to me that we can't separate the price He paid in dying without understanding the price He paid in coming to Earth to pay that price.

God with Us

God the Father placed within His hands His
only Son,
and with a tear He said to Him, "I have to send
you down.
"If you won't go then tell me who will save
their broken lives?
"Without you, Son, all will be lost," as more
tears swelled in His eyes.

"I love you, Son but you must go to live and
die with man,
"you know that it's the only way to save them
from their sin."
For a lonely moment the Son wept with His Father
they couldn't bear to be apart but love was crying
louder.
The Son stood in His Father's palm and they
embraced each other,
Jesus said, "I'm ready now to do your will,
My Father."
Gabriel was sent to tell the virgin who she
would carry,
as the Father blew a kiss, Jesus was placed in Mary.
So the Christmas story is told of angels, shepherds,
and stars, but Jesus Christ was really sent to live in
hearts like ours.
So ponder the true meaning of Christmas while you
celebrate His birth,
Emmanuel means "God with us," that's how much you
were worth!

Kim Strootman

Day 11

We all face times of struggle, doubt, pain, and temptation. One thing to be careful of during these painful times is to keep ourselves out of situations that might cause us to fall. Temptation may come, but if we're wise, we will remove ourselves from tempting situations and people who are potentially dangerous to us at the time. If you find yourself attracted to someone and you or that person is married, don't spend a lot of time with that person. If you're in a position where you have to, you may consider finding a new job, changing schools, or church classes you're in or whatever it takes to remove yourself from them. It is a recipe for disaster if you don't. It's not easy but you will be glad you made the change.

Many families are torn apart by affairs that could have been avoided.

Kim Strootman

Fantasies

Fantasies are only lies that make you want to sin,
at first they lift and pick you up then slam you down again.
When the stakes seem really high like taking on a lover,
it's like a blanket on your eyes and you can't see the cover.
You may satisfy your flesh but you'll sacrifice your Spirit,
when God says stop as clear as day—can you even hear it?
You think you're lonely now, my friend, if you give up this
fight, everyone will label you so please walk in the light.
Even so, they can not know the torment you endured,
so give up all those fantasies or your fall will be sure.

Day 12

Sometimes in life we feel isolated and lonely; however, if we accept Jesus as Lord of our life, we are not alone. Proverbs 18:24 says that we have a friend that sticks closer than a brother. We can trust that God is always with us, even when we feel like we're totally alone. Deuteronomy 31:6 also says, "I will never leave you or forsake you." Invite God into every situation you encounter in life—good and bad. He will take those times of isolation and loneliness and heal your soul if you let Him.

Loneliness

Sometimes there is a loneliness that seeps down
in my soul,
in coldness I seek warmth but there isn't any coal.
Though lonely for companionship I seem to search
in vain,
my heart begins to cry, finding solace in the rain.
When those I love have hurt me though I've
overlooked so much,
there is a healing balm in the Holy Spirit's touch.
Melting in His presence filling in the lonely space,
God's love reaches in bringing comfort in its place.

Day 13

Have you ever wondered how someone you know can simply walk away from God, church, friends, and family? It is heartbreaking to watch someone destroy their lives and the lives of others around them through selfish acts of desertion. Hebrews 5:12–14, which is my inspiration to write this poem, gives us a glimpse why this happens. Some people *digress* in their walk with the Lord. How does this happen? When we don't keep moving forward in our walk with God, reading His word, praying, and attending church as an active participant, we begin to revert to being a "baby" Christian.

According to this scripture, we should be eating solid food by now, but we're back to drinking milk again! It is never too late to wake up, turn ourselves around, and return to our relationship with God. Our world is full of distractions, and spending daily time with God is a commitment, but life is so much richer when our priorities are in order!

Kim Strootman

The Tree

There once was a tree that stood strong and brave,
through the seasons, it's strong branches would wave.
Nothing could deter this strong tree's growth
then something happened to affect its health.
When the time came for the healthy tree to eat,
it decided, "I don't need food to grow, I'll just
eat a treat."

Then time came for water so the roots would not dry,
the tree said, "I'm not thirsty and spread his branches wide."
No water could penetrate to feed thirsty ground,
his acorns fell dry and lifeless all around.
One winter day while feeling sick and cold,
the tree began to ponder things he had once been told.
The older, wiser trees encouraged him as he grew. "Don't
forget to eat your food so you will not grow weak,"
another said, "Water is important so your roots
can go down deep."
As time marched on the tree decided he knew best,
when the time came to eat or drink he simply took a rest.
Now looking back upon this foolishness he cried,
"Lord, please forgive me, I'm dying inside!"
God blew a wind upon him and then He said, "Now eat,
and don't forget to drink when rain falls at your feet!"
As the tree grew strong, he taught seedlings as they grew,
"Remember always to eat and drink. There's a story of a foolish
tree I would like to tell you…"

Day 14

I have the best sisters in the world, but even if you don't have a physical sister, you can have friends that are just like sisters. Some of my closest sister friends are those I've met in church Sunday school classes. If you are not in a smaller setting at your church where you can make friends and have fellowship time other than church, take my advice and do it; it's really worth it! Ask if your church has Sunday school classes, cell groups, or women or men classes or groups. Whether you're a man or a woman, good Christian friendships are imperative to help us grow and stay connected. Try it; you'll like it!

Sisters

Friends for life no matter
the weather,
silent companions when we
can't be together.
Dining and talking, laughter
fills the air,
a special knowing when the other
needs prayer.
Through life's ups and downs we'll
be together,
it is my privilege to call you
my sister.

Day 15

Having experienced betrayal before in different forms, I decided to write "Judas Kiss." When you experience betrayal, it is very painful and gives you some insight as to how Jesus must have felt to be betrayed by Judas. The most painful part was the kiss. Judas chose to give Jesus over to His enemies by the highest greeting—a kiss on the cheek. Psalm 55:12–14 describes this perfectly. What really hurt was that a friend and companion, not an enemy, did this to me. Hopefully, we will learn how to be a better friend to others in the future through the injustices that we have gone through in the past. This is found in Psalm 55:12–14 (NIV), "If an enemy were insulting me, I could endure it; if a foe were raising himself against me, I could hide from him. But it is you, a man like myself, my companion, my close friend, with whom I once enjoyed sweet fellowship as we walked with the throng at the house of God"

Judas Kiss

Betrayal is a nasty act that leaves you feeling used,
no matter what the reason the betrayed has been abused.
When someone's been disloyal, there's one way to make it right,
forgive and give it to the Lord—don't retaliate and fight!
When hurt turns into anger what are we supposed to do?
Get alone and pray—God is always there for you.
He is ever present for the one who needs Him most,
if you'll keep your heart pure, your enemy is toast!

Day 16

Reflecting on a Thomas Kincaid museum filled with lovely pictures of cottages and beautiful garden scenes, this poem came to me. As you read this poem, I hope you will think back on a fond childhood memory as I did when I wrote it. A familiar smell—wisteria, a rose bush, or maybe bread baking in your grandmother's oven. Remember the roads you traveled to get to your grandparents' house, the yard you played in, a best friend. Let yourself be transported in recollection of good memories from your past and those times when your gifts or talents became evident. The awkward moments that shaped where you were heading.

If you have strayed far away from your dreams, gifts, or calling by life's demands and routine, dream again. Consider what you're doing with your life and ask yourself, what should I be doing with my life? "His divine power has given us everything we need for a godly life through our knowledge of him who called us by his own glory and goodness" (2 Pet. 1:3, NIV).

Kim Strootman

The Visit

Sit back and take a journey to a different place and time,
it seems to have no meaning and you're questioning the rhyme.
A gentle summer breeze begins to blow upon your skin,
you're not quite sure but this could be a dream that you are in.
Walking up, a dirt path, grass, and trees on every side,
a garden gate is standing that shadows cannot hide.

You walk upon the pathway to a house you've seen before,
through a door that's waiting, familiar scents from long ago.
The smells bring precious memories of a time set in your past,
others may wonder why you're here but you don't have to ask.
For now you're standing right upon a place long been forgotten,
a time where gift and soul shook hands you knew this was
your calling.
It may have hurried by you so you didn't think it real,
but looking back you see it, just reach out, and you can feel.
Listen to the child within. See the moment and the place,
in your hand lies a golden strand if that memory you will trace.
For in your hand was placed a pearl for you to grasp and hold,
it's your turn now to follow your dream,
make it become your own.
The sun hits your eyes as you awake tears streaming down
your face,
your questions here were answered in His visit at this place!

Day 17

Psalm 139:7–10 is a beautiful picture of how close God is to us. Through every situation in life, God is right there with us. He walks with us through every high and low in life. Through the darkest times in my life, I knew I was not alone. It is comforting to know that when we feel all alone and we're walking through very rough times, God doesn't leave us. Where can I go from your Spirit? Here's what Psalm 139:7–10 (NIV) says, "Where can I flee from your presence? If I go up to the heavens, you are there; if I make my bed in the depths, you are there. If I rise on the wings of the dawn, if I settle on the far side of the sea, even there your hand will guide me, your right hand will hold me fast."

Guiding Light

Darkness comes in many forms but
can't steal God from me,
Carefully he guides me through
whatever kind of sea.
Even when I try to run God's there
to light my way,
Gently tugging at my heart this love's
a constant stay.
When darkness falls I will not hide for
this I've learned is true,
my darkness is as light to him, I know
He'll see me through.

Day 18

Several years ago, my family was together for the Christmas holidays. As I drove up at my parent's home, my father came out to meet me. Directly upon seeing him, my heart sank into my stomach. He was so thin I couldn't believe it. As the holiday progressed, we discovered that my father was very sick and would be having surgery within a few months. I had some precious moments with my dad that Christmas. At times we just sat together, holding hands and sitting close. On our last day before traveling home, my mom, sisters, and I went shopping. I ran into a cute lion tree ornament. I heard the Lord say to me, "Buy the ornament. You'll want a memory of this Christmas." I bought the ornament, and we all returned home from the holidays.

Unfortunately, my father had a major stroke after surgery, and by Good Friday I was attending his funeral. Every year as I put that lion ornament on my tree, I thank God for my precious memories of my dad. I also thank Him for telling me to buy the ornament that has forever locked that last Christmas with my dad in my mind. This scripture reminds me how much God loves us, "He heals the brokenhearted and binds up their wounds" (Ps. 147:3, NIV).

Kim Strootman

Grief to Gold

Time for tears, time for pain,
time for joy and healing rain.
Things may come and things may go,
but you can have a Rock of hope!
Sit down, let Him cleanse your soul,
make inner healing your ultimate goal.
Sufferings we go through bring God
close to earth,
hold on tight with all you're worth.

Don't say, "I should be over this by now,"
rest in Him—He'll show you how.
God has given you a heritage of memories
those times can outweigh the tough,
time will turn memories to strands of gold
for the Lord is big enough!

Kim Strootman

Day 19

After the terrible tsunami that devastated many Asian countries, especially Indonesia and Thailand, I wrote this. At the time of the tsunami, a natural disaster was running parallel with some things in my life that God was dealing with in me. I had a "natural disaster" of sorts at the same time this natural disaster was taking place. As I looked upon the faces of those who were wailing on the beaches, I related to them. Researching the word *wailing*, I found a profound description that it could also be termed, "singing," as in a loud groan. In my own life, I was crying out for relief of a different kind. You know the old saying, "Be careful what you pray for"? I had been praying for several years to God to change me.

I knew there was something deep inside me that needed healing, but I didn't realize just how much. As God began answering my prayers, it was hard to face, and I didn't even know at the time that's what was going on. In time by taking me through it, He brought me to a very healthy place. Now I say, "*Don't* be careful of what you pray for"; God always has our best interest at heart. Just be prepared for what He will do!

In 1 John 1:9 (NIV), it says, "If we confess our sins, he is faithful and just and will forgive us our sins and purify us from all unrighteousness".

Asia Is Singing

Ocean waves swelling, breaking on shores,
unaware multitudes about to be swarmed.
Water floods shorelines, hotels and houses,
cars and businesses inundating the masses.
Babies ripped from Mother's arms,
thousands drown in the sea,
some grateful for their miracle, loved ones found alive,
others ask, "Why couldn't that be mine?"

Every face desolate, every face bewildered,
may Nala rise up and bring forth her splendor.
To those hit so hard may supplies reach
your borders,
let food and water be plentiful, disease die with odors.
Many are mourning, souls are left bleeding,
give ear to her cries, Lord; Asia is singing.

Kim Strootman

Day 20

Waking up to a radio announcement one winter day, I heard the sweet cancellation of schools and businesses due to a winter storm. I couldn't help but feel giddy and elated at the prospect of an unplanned day off and being stuck in the house!

As I drank hot coffee listening to more reports of closings and finally getting a call from work saying, "Don't come in," this poem came to me. I, of course, wrote it in my pajamas in bed! This scripture tells us God really does want us to enjoy our life, "So I commend the enjoyment of life, because nothing is better for a man under the sun than to eat and drink and be glad. Then joy will accompany him in his work all the days of the life God has given him under the sun" (Eccles. 8:15, NIV).

Snow

Waking up feeling cold, some smells new, some smells old,
winter's kiss upon my skin, is this a dream that I'm still in?
Stumbling to the coffeepot I view the falling snow,
taken aback a smile cracks; does this mean I have nowhere
to go?
I quickly pour the coffee praying under snow is ice,
I'd love to just stay home today—boy would that be nice!
Reports confirm my deepest wish, "Don't drive unless
you must."
I cancel my day, relaxing away watching fresh snow as it dusts.

Day 21

In these uncertain times where jobs are scarce and we must be frugal, let's be sure to keep our hearts in the right place during the holidays. There are many things we can do to build fond memories that costs little to no money at all. Among the list of things to do is driving around, looking at Christmas lights, popping popcorn, and watching a movie at home or choosing from a myriad of free concerts or plays going on during the holidays at churches, schools, and parks. This can be a very precious time with our families and friends as we keep focused on what really matters. Ecclesiastes 3:1 (NIV) says, "There is a time for everything, and a season for every activity under the heavens."

Less Is More

The season's fast approaching and countdown is on,
I realize more fully how many years I've run.
In the past I've wanted things perfectly in tact,
this year there's less to use, it's important how I act.
Squeezed into this bubble where I'm counting every dime,
we're learning to be frugal, putting emphasis on time.
This year I'll put the Lord where I thought He was already,
not in gifts or feasting but in time He should be getting.
My prayer is that my children will learn this while
they're young,
to emphasize Lord Jesus Christ; the birthday of God's son!

Day 22

My nephew Kelly was in Iraq for about two years. During this time, I began to think about what it must be like to be somewhere that was the complete opposite of the American idea of Christmas and what families go through during that time. So many foreign feelings were present: wishing he could be home, what he was feeling, and concern for his mom and dad. There were new elements to Christmas that I hadn't experienced before that spurred me to write this poem—praying for a loved one's safety during that time and knowing he was so very far away.

Christmas in Iraq

A blistering wind is blowing
in the desert heat,
missile blasts are falling
where at night our children sleep.
Fighting for our country, fighting
for their lives,
dear God keep our loved ones safe
by day and through the night.

In sand instead of snow
missing family and friends,
let our dear ones know
that we are with them to the end.

"A thousand may fall at your side,
ten thousand at your right hand;
but it shall not come near you" (Psalm 91:7, NIV).

Kim Strootman

Day 23

After the attacks on the World Trade Center in New York, the media began calling the place of impact and complete devastation ground zero. I remember being so deeply touched by the lack of life there—a crater in the ground with nothing but debris. Seeing the correlation with the complete and utter devastation we sometimes go through in life, I couldn't help but think of nature. When a fire burns the ground and all vegetation seems hopelessly lost, inevitably, new life always springs up. Give yourself time, and you too will find new life springing up from your "ground zero."

Ground Zero

Standing at ground zero is
the perfect place to be.
Though devastation's all around,
up is all you see.
Tragedy left you here in pain but this
is where it ends,
healing arises with new hopes new life now begins.
In this place of grief and hurt you'll find
impenetrable calm,
for even in the darkest night God still speaks
to your storms.
Look down among the ashes, a green stem comes into view,
at ground zero life comes gently just to rescue you!

Day 24

This is a light-hearted poem about the things I've observed about holidays. Being with our families and making memories is a very special time in our lives.

Cocoa

2 tbs. cocoa powder
2 tbs. sugar
1 c. milk
1/8 tsp. vanilla extract (optional)
Pinch of salt

1. Mix cocoa, salt, and sugar together and set aside the mixture.

2. Heat milk in a saucepan to just before boiling on the stovetop and add cocoa mixture.

3. Sit back and enjoy!

Kim Strootman

Holiday

Mothers cook with pots and pans,
children off to sleepy land.
Fathers sit and watch their games,
are our animals insane?
Smells are wafting in the air,
as the meal we cooks prepare.
Something's magic 'bout this season,
doesn't take a genius to know the reason.
Cold winds blow keeping families inside,
playing games and spending time.
Holidays are special—do you know why?
When we're together love abides!

Day 25

Have you ever wondered when life would slow down to allow you the time to find special projects where you could be a witness for Christ? Being light and salt to the world comes in many ways and many forms. A lot of times it comes in our daily life's busyness; being an example to coworkers and showing patience and kindness to people who are difficult can be a great form of showing Christian love. This poem celebrates everyday life. We spread the Gospel every day, everywhere we go: work, school, shopping centers, etc.

Slowing down to be an example of Christ is very important even when we're in a huge hurry. I tend to be a "point A to point B" person, getting one task done and moving on to the next quickly. Ask yourself this question the next time you're tempted to "push" people out of your way to get on with your day: why do I feel that my day is more important than this person's? Let's make it our mission to go about doing good to others and spreading the Gospel in word as well as our actions.

The Mission

God's great commission Jesus's very
last words,
"Go tell the Gospel Let the Good
News be heard.
Many are hurting and many
are weak,
the stronger your vessel the louder
you'll speak.

Some reach the world by the droves
and the masses,
some will reach students while sitting
in classes.
Others will witness during employment
tasks,
housewives carry Jesus wherever He
asks.
Our light should grow brighter as this
world grows darker,
God's love and mercy should be
our marker.
So go about life as God's mouth, feet
and hands,
let your light shine as you boldly stand."

Day 26

The past year seems to have been a difficult one for me. I've been through many experiences: heartbreaks, broken dreams, a daughter moving far across the country, hurt feelings with close friends, and changes in my job. When things come at us so fast that we're still reeling from the last thing as the next one is bombarding us, how do we handle it?

The real test of what's inside us surfaces. When that happens, we have a choice to make: will we *demand* our rights even if we're not in the right or will we *humble* ourselves, evaluate our heart and actions, and make the changes in ourselves? This poem was birthed at the end of many struggles, where the last one was the so-called "straw that broke the camel's back." I came to the end of myself and found freedom in giving up my right to be right. Philippians 4:8 (NIV) tells us, "Finally, brothers, whatever is true, whatever is noble, whatever is right, whatever is pure, whatever is lovely, whatever is admirable—if anything is excellent or praiseworthy—think about such things".

Kim Strootman

Laying Down My Right

I went through a season of hurt and pain,
wanting old friendships to remain the same.
Anger and frustrations were taking a toll,
between us they made an invisible hole.
Emotions boiled and tempers flared,
as I falsely told myself that I didn't care.
As a faceoff began and both sides stood tall,
Jesus asked me, "Will you let your rights fall?"
He caught me by surprise—wasn't He on *my* side?
Gently He reminded me, "You're acting in pride."
Picking up my Bible it was clear where I strayed,
at His feet I repented lightening my way.

Burdens lifted as I walked in forgiveness,
healing my heart from the offences.
God's will required that I give up this fight,
I had to evaluate: was my attitude right?
That's always the standard that tells me the truth,
sometimes to win there are things you must lose.

Each one should test his own actions. Then he can
take pride in himself, without comparing himself
to somebody else.

—Galatians 6:4 (NIV)

Kim Strootman

Day 27

We live in ever-changing times, but let not your heart be troubled! God has a plan to sustain His people no matter what we see going on in the world if we will only listen and obey.

Every year I write a poem at Christmastime to send to my family and friends. There was a lot going on in 2009 that didn't seem positive. As I began to pray about what to write, God dropped this poem in my heart and 1 Kings 17:8–16 to go with it. As I read the scripture, I saw the correlation of what difficult times the widow of Zarephath was also living through. When she was asked to give Elijah a little water and to make him a small cake, it was literally all she had left for her and her son.

What she didn't realize, however, was that God had looked down on her desolation and was prepared to help her out. By being obedient to make God's prophet the last cake she had, her jar of oil and bin of flour never ran out until the Lord once again sent rain on the earth! See how God provides!

Kim Strootman

Noonday Sun

In this time of turmoil when the world is in a spin,
we're covered in God's hands if we'll only let Him in.
Creative ideas—a must in these ever changing times,
Creator of the Universe wants to sanctify your mind.
He'll give us what we need as we give to Him our best,
priceless to the Master, but our lives are up for test.
Let not your heart be troubled but please renew your mind,
put here for a purpose—don't forget to shine!
Blooms prove plants are healthy so let the Gardner prune,
soon you will be blooming just like sunshine at noon!

Day 28

Busyness can steal moments, days and even years from our lives and make us ineffective as a Christian. We may have jobs and various responsibilities, but if we are so busy that we aren't looking around to see who we can bless while we're "doing" life, we are missing it.

I speak from experience. I'm a wife and mother and have a full-time job. I've been working full time for three years now, and I realized a few months ago that I was moving through life, rushing in and out of stores putting *my* life first and not looking at anyone or helping anyone on a daily basis.

We don't realize how hard we can become when we are living life as the world and not as a believer. Oh sure, I had certain people I was trying to help and commitments here and there, but what about *daily*? I decided to quit rushing in and out without taking notice of others around me.

Now, my whole perspective has changed, and my goals in life have changed too. First, we are God's, we've been bought with a price, and we have to show it to a needy world!

Seeds

Seeds are meant for scattering,
for sowing in the earth,
pray for the "soil" you meet each day
to be "good ground"; not just "dirt."
What will you plant in people today,
impatience and contention?
You could plant peace and love,
it's really your decision.
Our daily walk through life has a
powerful sway,
most of the time we mistake it for
an ordinary day.

"Lord, teach me to sow good things
in those you bring my way,
help me plant smiles, conversation and
time each and every day."

Day 29

When the movie *The Passion of the Christ* came out, I felt compelled to invite a friend of mine to go with me to see it. I had already seen it once with my husband.

When I got to the theatre, my friend hadn't arrived yet, and there was a line to get in to all the movies showing that day. The gentleman in front of me started up a conversation with me and asked which movie I was going to see. He began asking some very important questions concerning Jesus, His life and death, and the price he paid. It was like we had a captive audience while we discussed this. At the end of the conversation the man said something very profound. He said, "Isn't that what He came for anyway?"

I echoed his response with, "Yes, that's exactly why He came—to die for us." Since we had already discussed the reason He died and what it meant for mankind, it was the perfect way to end this in front of so many. You could have heard a pin drop. As soon as we finished, my friend showed up, and the line began moving. I thank God for those moments we get to share His love to people in an unusual setting!

The Passion

Bruised for our iniquities stinging
with pain,
Jesus was stricken again and again.
No outward beauty to draw us
to Him,
with His blood He purchased
mankind from sin.
Beauty for ashes, comfort for pain,
just a few blessings of the Great
Exchange.

Consider today how you're
living your life,
for you were His passion;
The passion of Christ!

Day 30

After a year of suffering and pain, both physical and emotional, I wrote this poem. It commemorates the feelings I felt during and after this time. There are times in our lives when we have to look in the mirror and examine ourselves—our motives for doing what we do. If we are truly honest with ourselves, we will reach that time when we realize we need to step down or step back to enter a deeper level of healing, change of direction, or simply go back to the one-on-one relationship with God before taking on another task.

My prayer is that when you reach your moment of truth, you will have the courage to step down from your position to follow after your first love—Jesus Christ.

The Master's Teacup

Once a lovely teacup on a shelf of often use,
fell in shattered pieces from its high and
needed place.
The cup so brutally broken couldn't hold a
drop of tea,
"Can I ever now be used again?" was this
teacup's plea.
Alone and on a separate shelf watching other
teacups work,
while in a dozen pieces he was being healed
from hurt.

As time went on he didn't care to leave the
lonely space,
he found worth in the Master's hand as He
did gently mend each piece.
Finally the day came when the cup was
whole and sure,
stronger now than ever for the time he
took to cure.
However there had been a change
in teacup's inner stature,
his worth was not in holding tea but being
held by Master.